Basil Hall Chamberlain

The Serpent With Eight Heads

Basil Hall Chamberlain

The Serpent With Eight Heads

ISBN/EAN: 9783744704175

Printed in Europe, USA, Canada, Australia, Japan

Cover: Foto ©Thomas Meinert / pixelio.de

More available books at **www.hansebooks.com**

Japanese Fairy Tale Series. No. 9.

The Serpent With Eight Heads.

Told in English.

by B. H. Chamberlain.

Published

by the KOBUNSHA,

日本昔噺第九號

八頭ノ大蛇
定價金十五錢

英國王堂チヤムバレイン先生編述

明治十九年十月十六日版權免許

同　十一月　出版

東京府平民

印刷人　長谷川武次郎
東京府麹町區飯田町二丁目

出版所　弘文社

The
Serpent
with Eight Heads.

id you ever hear the story of the Eight-Headed Serpent? If not, I will tell it to you. It is rather a long one, and we must go a good way back to get to the beginning of it.

In fact, we must go back to the beginning of the world.

After the world had been created, it became the property of a very powerful fairy; and when this fairy was about to die, he divided it between his two boys and his girl.

The girl called Ama, was given the sun; the eldest boy, called Susano,

was

given the sea;

and the second boy,

whose name I forget, was given the moon. Well, the Moon-Boy behaved himself properly; and you can still see his jolly round face on a clear night when the moon is full. But Susano was very angry and disappointed at having nothing but the cold wet sea to live in. So up he rushed into the sky, burst into the beautiful room inside the sun, where his sister was sitting with her maidens weaving gold and silver dresses, broke their spindles, trampled upon their work, and in short did all the mischief he could, and frightened the

poor maids to death. As for Ama, she ran away as fast as she could, and hid herself in a cave on the side of a mountain full of rocks and crags. When she had got into the cave and had shut the door, the whole world became pitch-dark. For she was the fairy who ruled the sun, and could make it shine or not as she chose. In fact, some people say that the light of the sun is really nothing else than the brightness of her own bright eyes. Anyhow, there was great trouble over her disappearance. What was to be done to make the world light again?

All sorts of plans were tried. At last, knowing that she was curious and always liked to see every thing that was going on, the other fairies got up a dance outside the door of the cave.

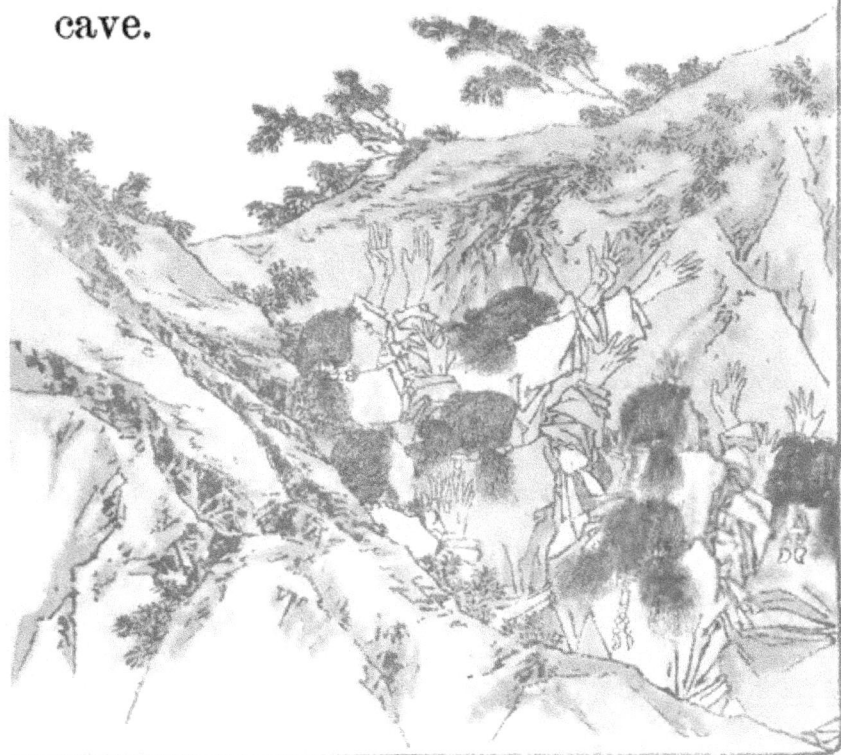

When Ama heard the noise of
the dancing and singing and laugh-
ing, she could not help opening the
door a tiny bit, in order to peep
through the chink at the fun the
other fairies were having. This was
just what they had been watching for.
"Look here!" cried they; "look at this
new fairy more beautiful than your-
self!" and therewith they thrust
forward a mirror. Ama did not
know that the face in the mirror
was only the reflection of her
own; and, more and more curious
to know who the new fairy could be,

she **ventured** outside **the** door, where **she was** caught hold of by **the** other fairies, **who piled** up the entrance **of the** cave **with** big rocks, **so that no** one could ever go into it again. **Seeing** that she had been tricked **into coming out of** the cave, and that there was no use in sulking **any** longer, Ama agreed to go back **to** the sun and shine upon the world **as before,** provided her brother were punished **and** sent away in disgrace; for really **he** was not safe to live with. **This was** done. Susa **was** beaten to within an inch of his life,

and expelled
from the society of the other fairies,
with orders never to
show himself
again.

So poor Susa, having been turned out of fairy-land, was obliged to come down to the earth. While walking one day on the bank of a river, he happened to see an old man and an old woman with their arms round their young daughter, and crying bitterly.

"What is the matter?" asked Susa.
"Oh!" said, they, their voice choked
with sobs, "we used to have eight
daughters. But in a marsh near our

hut there lives a huge Eight-Headed Serpent, who comes out once every year, and eats up one of them. We have now only one daughter left, and to-day is the day when the Serpent will come to eat her, and then we shall have none. Please good Sir! Can you not do something to help us"?—"Of course," answered Susa; "it will be quite easy. Do not be sad any longer. I am a fairy, and I will save your daughter." So he told them to brew some beer, and showed them how to make a fence with eight gates in it, and a wooden stand inside each gate, and a large vat of beer on each stand. This they did; and just as all had been arranged in the way Susa had bidden them, the Serpent came. So huge was he, that his body trained over eight hills and eight valleys as he wriggled along. But as he had eight heads, he also had eight noses, which made him able to smell eight times as quickly as any other creature. So, smelling the beer from afar off, he at once glided towards it, went inside the fence, dipped one

of his heads into each of the eight vats, and drank and drank and drank, till he got quite tipsy. Then all his heads dropped down fast asleep; and Susa, jumping up from the hole where he had lain hidden, drew his sword, and cut them all off. He cut the body to pieces too. But, strange to say, when cutting the tail, the blade of his sword snapped. It had struck against something hard. As the Serpent was now dead, there was no danger in going up to it, and finding out what the hard thing was. It turned out to be itself a sword all set with precious stones,—the most beautiful sword you ever saw. Susa took the sword, and married the beautiful young girl; and he was very kind to her, although he had been so rude to his elder sister. They spent the rest of their lives in a beautiful palace, which was built on purpose for them; and the old father and mother lived there too.

When the old father and mother, and Susa and his wife had all died, the sword was handed down to their children, and grandchildren; and it now belongs to the Emperor of Japan, who looks upon it as one of his most precious treasures.

———————

The Kobunsha's Japanese Fairy Tale Series.

Published by the KOBUNSHA, 2, Minami Saegicho, TOKYO

www.ingramcontent.com/pod-product-compliance
Lightning Source LLC
Chambersburg PA
CBHW032144080426
42733CB00008B/1202